It is often said that there are a lot of Ojisan—grown men who are not one's father—in Higuchi's manga. That's because I like Ojisan. I feel affection toward their balding heads, as well as their wrinkles. I see pride in their stubborn attitudes. I find love in their words, although not often spoken. Of course, the world is not filled with only the type I just described. Nonetheless, those who've lived many years possess a drama of their own. Manga (as well as movies and TV dramas) are fun when a tasteful *Oyaji* appears! It is my policy to include Ojisan type men in my manga.

- Daisuke Higuchi

Daisuke Higuchi's manga career began in 1992 when the artist was honored with third prize in the 43rd Osamu Tezuka Award. In that same year, Higuchi debuted as creator of a romantic action story titled **Itaru**. In 1998, **Weekly Shonen Jump** began serializing **Whistle!** Higuchi's realistic soccer manga became an instant hit with readers and eventually inspired an anime series, debuting on Japanese TV in May of 2002. The artist is currently working on a yet-to-be-published new series.

WHISTLE!
VOL. 6: BE THERE

The SHONEN JUMP Graphic Novel Edition

STORY AND ART BY
DAISUKE HIGUCHI

English Adaptation/Marv Wolfman
Translation/Naomi Kokubo
Touch-up Art & Lettering/Jim Keefe
Cover, Graphics & Layout/Sean Lee
Editor/Megan Bates

Managing Editor/Elizabeth Kawasaki
Director of Production/Noboru Watanabe
Vice President of Publishing/Alvin Lu
Vice President & Editor in Chief/ Yumi Hoashi
Sr. Director of Acquisitions/Rika Inouye
Vice President of Sales & Marketing/Liza Coppola
Publisher/Hyoe Narita

Printed in the U.S.A.

Published by VIZ, LLC
P.O. Box 77010
San Francisco, CA 94107

SHONEN JUMP Graphic Novel Edition
10 9 8 7 6 5 4 3 2 1
First printing, June 2005

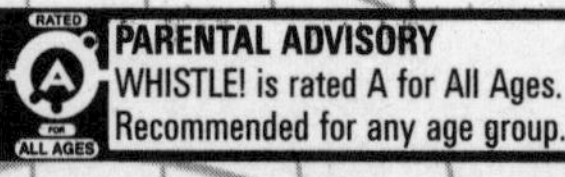

THE WORLD'S MOST POPULAR MANGA
SHONEN JUMP GRAPHIC NOVEL
www.shonenjump.com

www.viz.com

Vol. 6

BE THERE

Story and Art by Daisuke Higuchi

CHARACTERS

SHŌ
KAZAMATSURI

● JOSUI JUNIOR HIGH
SOCCER TEAM
FORWARD

KŌ
KAZAMATSURI

YŪKO
KATORI

TATSUYA
MIZUNO

● JOSUI JUNIOR HIGH
SOCCER TEAM
MIDDLE FIELDER

SOUJŪ MATSUSHITA

FORMER JAPAN LEAGUE PLAYER

JOSUI JUNIOR HIGH COACH

RYOICHI TENJO

KOKUBU SECOND JUNIOR HIGH SOCCER TEAM

FORWARD

SHIGEKI SATŌ

JOSUI JUNIOR HIGH SOCCER TEAM

FORWARD

STORY

Not wanting to give up his dream, Shō Kazamatsuri, a substitute player at Musashinomori, transfers schools to Josui Junior High, so he can play soccer.

With Soujū Matsushita, a former Japan League player, as their new coach, the Josui Junior High soccer team starts their power retreat to prepare for the summer championship.

On the last day of the retreat, Josui Junior High has a practice match against Kokubu Second Junior High, and they finish the first half two to zero. However, during the second half, due to the overwhelming power of Ryoichi Tenjo, the FW of Kokubu Second Junior High, they lose two points, which ties their scores. By observing Ryoichi's characteristic movements, Sakura of Josui Junior High scores another point, but...

Vol. 6
BE THERE

STAGE.45 Solitary Profile

SHI-GEKI!
JOSUI SCORES THE THIRD POINT!
WAPP
YOU'RE GETTING A BETTER GRASP OF WHAT SOCCER'S ALL ABOUT, SHŌ.
IT WAS REALLY GOOD TO BE ABLE TO ASSIST ME JUST THEN.
Y'KNOW, AT FIRST I COULDN'T GET SERIOUS ABOUT A PRACTICE MATCH...
BUT I'M FINALLY GETTING MY HEAD AROUND IT.
GRABB
WELL, YOU REALLY HELPED ME.
I'M GOING TO PLAY HARD!
IT'S KINDA LATE TO DECIDE THAT NOW.

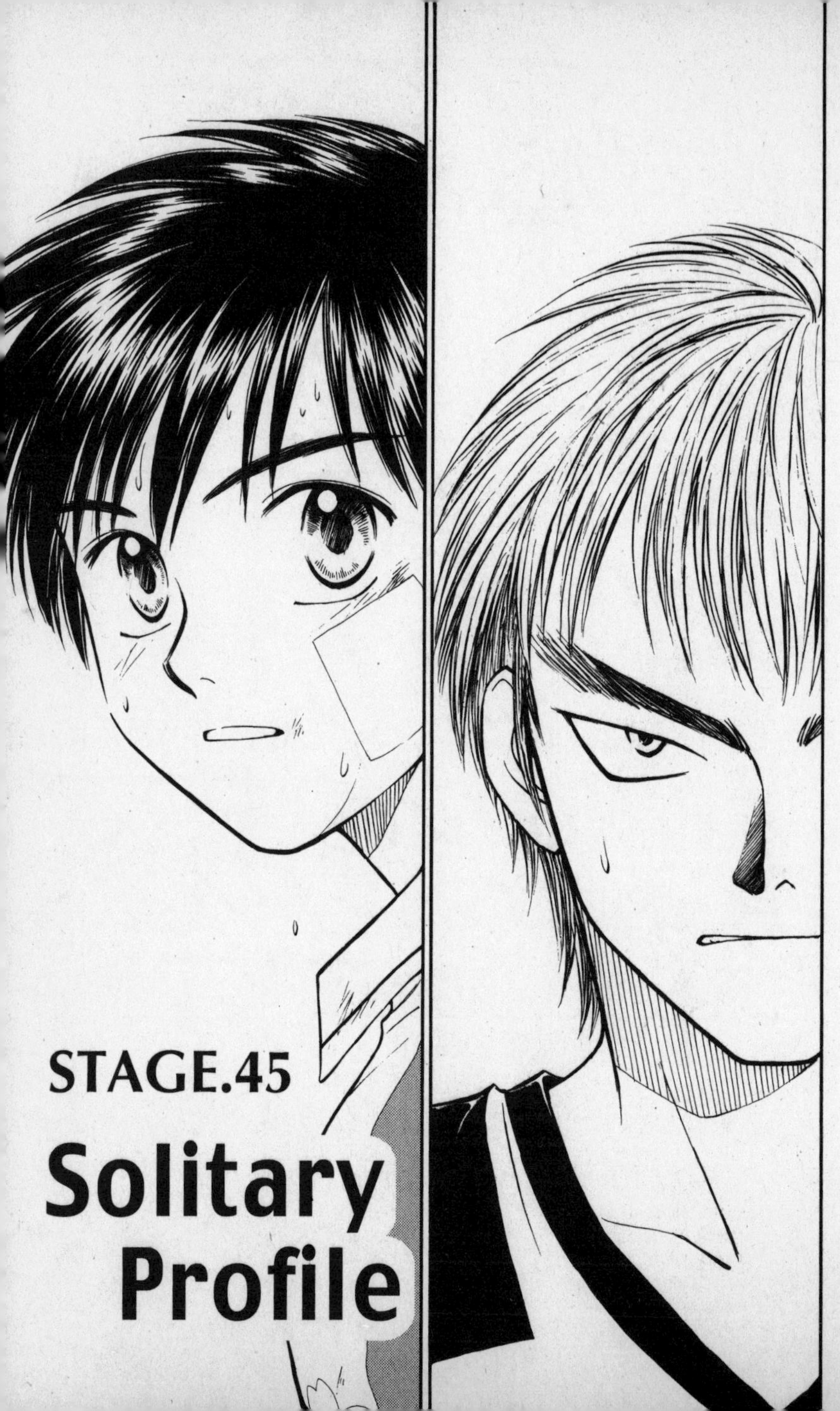

STAGE.45

Solitary Profile

GRIN
!
HMPH
I DON'T UNDERSTAND...
...HE PLAYS SOCCER LIKE HE'S IN PAIN.
I WONDER IF IT'S...
...NOT FUN FOR HIM.
9
...RYOICHI, SOCCER ISN'T SOME-THING ONE PLAYS ALONE.

BUT IF I PLAY AT THEIR LEVEL, I'LL NEVER MAKE IT.

TAP

TO BECOME A WORLD CLASS FW, I HAVE TO USE MY LEFT LEG AS WELL AS MY RIGHT.

ALTHOUGH I'M RIGHT-HANDED, I CAN CONTROL THOSE GUYS WITH MY LEFT LEG ALONE ...

THEY DON'T UNDERSTAND HOW GOOD I AM. BUT I CAN PROVE IT BY JUST USING MY LEFT LEG.

CAN YOU DO THAT?

YOU'RE AN INCREDIBLE PLAYER. YOU HAVE THE NATURAL TALENT TO BECOME A TOP PLAYER...

UNTIL YOU REALIZE IT...
...YOU WON'T EVEN WIN AGAINST JOSUI.
TAA'WHEEEET
I WON'T LOSE...
I WANT YOU TO DIVIDE INTO RED TEAMS AND WHITE FOR A MINI-GAME.
MUSASHINOMORI PRIVATE SCHOOL
NOT AGAINST THEM...

PASS!

IN AN ORDINARY SITUATION, I WOULD HAVE PASSED THE BALL.

BAM
I HAVE TO BE BETTER THAN THE REST.
BUT, MY GOAL IS THE WORLD ARENA.
IN A GAME LIKE THIS IF I CAN'T MAKE THE FINISHING SHOT, I WON'T MAKE IT TO THE WORLD.
I HAVE TO.
I HAVE TO MAKE THIS ON MY OWN.

ROAARRR

THERE ISN'T ANYONE ELSE SPECIAL IN THE OPPOSING TEAM OR IN MINE.
WA-TANA-BE...
FU-JISHI RO...
IBA RA-KI...
I THOUGHT THERE WAS NO DOUBT I'D BE SELECTED ...
TA-KE-DA...

...HAVE PASSED AS REGULAR PLAYERS. PLEASE PROCEED TO THE RECEPTION TO RECEIVE THE NECESSARY DOCUMENTS TO ENTER THE SCHOOL.

WHY WASN'T I...?
YOU, HUH ...?

YOU WERE PRETTY GOOD, BUT...
...THE COACH SAID YOU'RE NOT NEEDED FOR THE TEAM HE WANTS TO BUILD.

STILL, WE CAN'T DISMISS YOUR TALENT ...
...SO, I MADE SURE YOU CAN GET IN AS A SUBSTITUTE PLAYER.
...ME.
HUH?
HUH ?
YOU'RE JOKING ?!
ME? A SUB-STITUTE PLAYER !?
NO WAY I'D BE PART OF THAT.

I THINK HIS NAME IS TATSUYA MIZUNO...

HUH

HE REFUSED THE OFFER?

TATSUYA MIZUNO.

DEFENSE!
COVER EACH OTHER!
AND STOP HIM!
NORO!
KAORU !!
DON'T GIVE UP.
HE'S BEEN ANNOYING SINCE I FIRST MET HIM.
VIOLATED MY PRIVACY.
SHŌ.

HEH.
SO, JOSUI'S NO. 9 IS FROM MUSASHI-NOMORI.
YEAH. LAST TIME WE HAD A PRACTICE GAME I ASKED HIM ABOUT THE MUSASHI-NOMORI MATCH.
HE KEPT BREAKING THEIR SET-PLAY OPPORTUNITIES SO I ASKED HIM HOW HE KNEW...
I SEE. IF HE WAS AT MUSASHI-NOMORI, HE WOULD KNOW.
WHY DID HE GO TO JOSUI?
NO IDEA.
APPARENTLY, HE DECIDED ON HIS OWN ACCORD.
WHAT'S HIS NAME?
RYO-ICHI!?
JOSUI'S NO.9?
SHŌ...
AH.
TAP TAP
THAT SMALL GUY...
SHŌ...
...AND THAT'S TATSUYA ...!!

LET ME IN, COACH AMAMIYA.
THESE GUYS ARE HAPPY WITH SIMPLE ORGANIZED PLAY AT A JUNIOR HIGH LEVEL...
BUT I'LL SHOW THEM WHAT REAL PLAYING'S ABOUT.

TATSUYA TURNED DOWN MUSASHI-NOMORI EVEN THOUGH...
...HE WAS ACCEPTED.
AND SHŌ WAS AT MUSASHI-NOMORI...
...BUT HE THREW THAT AWAY.

BUT I'M...
...DIFFERENT. THEY'RE HAPPY TO PLAY SIMPLE SOCCER.

PASS...
...THE BALL!
PASS THE BALL!
PASS IT, RYO-ICHI!
I WON'T...

...BE DEFEATED ...
...BY YOU!
THE NO. 9 OF KOKUBU SECOND IS GOING TO SHOOT BETWEEN THE LEGS OF THE DF BLOCKING HIS LEFT LEG.
JOSUI

THE LAST TIME AROUND...
I FIGURED OUT HIS STRATEGY.
IF HE'S GOING TO SHOOT THROUGH THE LEGS, THIS IS THE ONLY COURSE.
COMPUTING THE SPEED OF THE BALL AND MY SPEED...
WAM
...WHAT'S LEFT IS...

KRANNNN
...THE TIMING!!

UNHUHHHH
GRRR
IT WON'T WORK AGAINST ME THE THIRD TIME!

DA-
ICHI!

KAA-RAMMM

LET'S
GO,
SHŌ!

LET'S GO! SHŌ!!
STAGE.46 Road to the Future
RYOICHI...
YAYYY! ♡

STAGE.46
Road to the Future
TAAA-WHEEET

JOSUI JUNIOR HIGH WINS.
THE GAME'S OVER. THREE TO TWO.

DID IT!
YOU IDIOT! I'M NOT LAUGHING. -HIC-
SOB SOB
I'M-- I'M CRYING.
-HIKKUP-
SNIFF SNIFF
LOCKER ROOM
WOW. RITZY! THEY'VE GOT SHOWER STOOLS!
SNIFF
SNIFF
MASATO, WHAT'S THAT WEIRD LAUGH?
I DIDN'T EXPECT -HIKKUP- TO BE ABLE TO PLAY...WASN'T SOMETHING I EXPECTED. AND I DID WELL -HIKKUP- AND TO TOP IT OFF, WE WON -HIKKUP- I'M SO GLAD...SO...GLAD.
WHIIW
THIS IS OUR FIRST VICTORY.
FWHOOSHHH
FWIISSHH
SHAA SHAA

WE DID IT!
YAY!
JOSH
I'VE GOT TO REMEMBER. ALWAYS WORK HARD.
THIS WAS A SHORT BUT EFFECTIVE RETREAT.
BUT I'M GLAD YOU WON.
LOCKER ROOM
GEEZ, YOU'RE TOO EXCITED. IF THE GUYS FROM KOKUBU SECOND HEARD YOU, THEY'D FEEL HORRIBLE.
HA HA HA HA
HEY? ANYONE SEE SHŌ?
IS HE LOST?
YOU'RE RIGHT.
HE'S NOT HERE.
SCRUB SCRUB
WHISHHH
MAN, THAT WAS A GREAT SHOWER.
WHAT'S UP, GUYS? YOU ALL SOUND WEIRD.

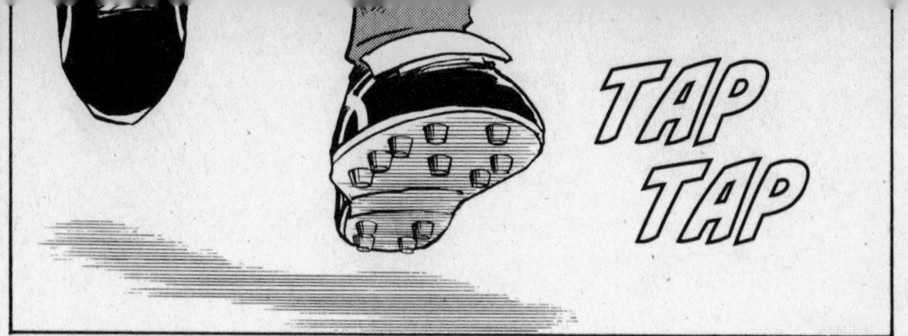

I LOST HIM.

WHERE DID HE GO?

OBAA-SAN... GRAND-MA...

MASTER RYOICHI.

ER-- WELL ...

I'M LOOKING FOR HIM...

DO YOU KNOW WHERE HE MIGHT BE?

IF YOU'RE TALKING ABOUT MASTER RYOICHI, HE'S PROBABLY ...
...SOME-WHERE HE CAN BE ALONE.
WHEN-EVER HE'S TROUBLED, HE DOES THAT.
OBAA-SAN, ER-- YOU'RE RYO-ICHI'S...
I USED TO BE HIS NANNY.
SO HOW OLD ARE YOU?
I'M-- I'M FOUR-TEEN.
OH. SO YOU'RE THE SAME AGE AS MY YOUNG MASTER.
WHAT? NO WAY!
PLEASE DO NOT THINK ILL OF MY YOUNG MASTER.
HE IS, IN FACT, A GENTLE SOUL.
ALSO, HE TRIES HARDER THAN THE OTHERS.
SHH. LET'S KEEP THIS A SECRET FROM YOUR FATHER.
WHOA! THANK YOU, KAZUE.
I WILL TREASURE IT.

AS HEIR OF THE TENJO GROUP, MASTER RYOICHI WAS ALWAYS FORCED TO SHOW RESULTS.
PEOPLE BELIEVE HE'S BEEN RAISED INDULGENTLY. BUT IT IS THE OPPOSITE.
SUCH BELIEFS LED TO MANY THREATS AND DEMANDS.
BEFORE I KNEW IT...
YOUNG MASTER, GIVE ME MONEY.
IF YOU DON'T ...
...HE TURNED INTO SOMEONE WHO RARELY LAUGHED.
AND EVER SINCE HE FAILED TO BE SELECTED AS A REGULAR AT MUSASHINOMORI...
...SOCCER, WHICH USED TO BE HIS ONLY COMFORT, BECAME HIS PROSECUTOR.
HOW COME HE FAILED?
HE TRIED FOR MUSASHI-NOMORI!?
I DO NOT KNOW. IT WAS HIS GOAL TO DEBUT IN THE WORLD ARENA, AND HE PLAYED IN A WAY THOUGHT TO BE SELFISH.
BUT SINCE THEN HE HAS DEMANDED...
...MORE OF HIMSELF THAN NECESSARY. HE'S PLACED HIGHER HURDLES AND CONTINUED TO PUSH HIMSELF HARDER.
IT WAS SO PAINFUL TO SEE.
COULD IT BE ...
...THE REASON WHY HE WAS PARTICULAR ABOUT HIS LEFT LEG DURING THE MATCH?
MY YOUNG MASTER IS RIGHT-HANDED.
JOSUI

READ THIS WAY

PLEASE BE KIND...
TO MY YOUNG MASTER.

KA-ZUE... KA-ZUE...
WHAT IS IT...
...YOUNG MASTER?

I, A THIRD GRADER, DEFEATED THE TEAM OF FOURTH GRADERS!
TEACHER COMPLIMENTED ME, SAYING I HAVE A TALENT.
WOW.

THAT'S WONDER-FUL.

HEH HEH

KAZUE, YOU LOOK HAPPY.
I'M HAPPY BECAUSE YOU LOOK HAPPY.
I DO?
YES.

I AM THE HAPPIEST WHEN I SEE YOU DOING YOUR BEST...
...AT WHAT YOU LOVE MOST.
THEN, I'LL TRY EVEN HARDER !!
I'M GOING TO BECOME A SOCCER PLAYER!

WRENCH

AT TIMES LIKE THIS, WHY DO I REMEMBER SOMETHING THAT HAPPENED SO LONG AGO?
AM I LOSING BELIEF IN MYSELF?
JUST BECAUSE I LOST A PRACTICE MATCH?
WHEN I FAILED TO BECOME A REGULAR AT MUSASHINOMORI...
WAIT!
...AND WHEN I WAS ORDERED...
...OUT OF THE GAME DURING THE SPRING CHAMPION-SHIP...
...I FELT ANGER, BUT...
...IT DIDN'T MAKE ME LOSE FAITH.
I TURNED EVERY RAGE I FELT INTO....
...ENERGY WHICH I USED TO IMPROVE.
SPLAP
DESPITE...
SO WHY...?

ONE CRIES WHEN THEY FEEL HUMILIATED.

A TEAR!?

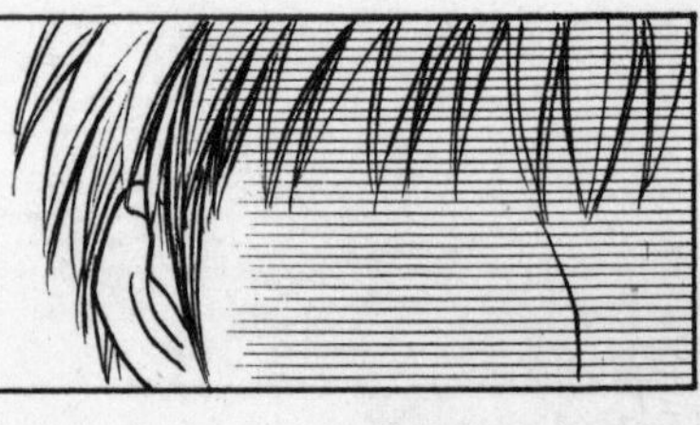

OOPS ...

S--SORRY!
...I DIDN'T MEAN TO...ER...I HAPPENED BY... I--I--I WAS LOOKING FOR ...

TRRIIIPPP

UN-HH-HH!
OHH-HHH!
AH-HHH!
GRAPP
TH--THANK YOU VERY MUCH.
WUNCHH
WHAT DO YOU WANT?
...
I--I WANTED TO SEE ... ...AND TALK ...TO YOU.
I'VE NEVER SEEN ANY-ONE SO INCREDIBLE.
WHAT'S SO INCREDIBLE ABOUT ME?
WHAT ...? ER--
YOUR POWER TO BREAK THROUGH ...
...TO ESTABLISH A DEFINITIVE CHANCE SINGLE-HANDEDLY. YOU'RE AN FW, BUT YOU'RE TOTALLY DIFFERE--

DON'T JOKE WITH ME!
YOU MOCK ME WHEN I LOST AGAINST YOU LOSERS?
I BET YOU CAME TO LAUGH AT ME!
NO... NO... THAT'S NOT WHAT I MEANT.
I HAVE AN ABILITY TO ESTABLISH A DEFINITIVE CHANCE SINGLE-HANDEDLY?
YEAH. RIGHT.
WHAT YOU'RE SAYING IS THAT I MONOPOLIZE THE BALL!
THEN ...
...WHY ARE YOU HERE? TO "COMFORT" ME?
'CAUSE THAT WOULD BE AN EVEN BIGGER INSULT.

I'M SORRY YOU THINK THAT BUT I REALLY THOUGHT YOU WERE INCREDIBLE.
HOW ELSE COULD I TELL YOU!?
国部二
I, ALSO ...
... WANT TO BECOME A PROFES-SIONAL PLAYER.
NO WAY.
IT'LL TAKE A MILLION YEARS.
MAY-BE.
IT WOULD HAVE. I MEAN, TILL NOW I ONLY VAGUELY WANTED TO BE ONE.
BUT THEN I MET YOU...

AND SINCE BEING LIKE YOU IS MY GOAL...
I CAN MAKE IT IF I DON'T GIVE UP.

IF I NEED TO HAVE YOUR SKILLS TO BE A PROFESSIONAL, THEN I'LL GET THEM.

AND IF I CAN'T BE A PROFESSIONAL UNLESS I'M BETTER THAN YOU, THEN I'LL BECOME BETTER.

NO MATTER HOW MANY YEARS IT TAKES.

I LOVE SOCCER ...
AND I CAN'T LET YOU BEAT ME.
JOS

GET LOST.
SHŌ KAZAMATSURI, HUH?
TAP
TAP
TAP
BOW
THERE YOU ARE.

WHERE WERE YOU? TRYING TO GET LEFT BEHIND?
HERE'S YOUR STUFF.
THANKS.
HAD THINGS TO DO.
HMM ...
GOING AFTER THEIR MANAGER, HUH?
NAH, THAT'S YOU.
POONK

LET'S GO.

THAT FW WHO JOINED HALFWAY THROUGH MADE THE GAME PRETTY CLOSE.
YEAH. TO BE HONEST, HE GOT ME TOTALLY SCARED.
DON'T KNOW IF WE WOULDA WON IF HE WAS PLAYING FROM THE START.
ME, TOO.
THERE'S NO WAY HE COULD BE THE SAME AGE AS US.

FIRST TIME I MET YOU, TATSUYA, I THOUGHT YOU WERE A REALLY GOOD PLAYER, BUT...

...RYOICHI SORT OF IS, TOO, IN A TOTALLY DIFFERENT WAY...

I GUESS THERE'S OTHER GREAT PLAYERS I HAVEN'T MET YET.

I WANT TO PLAY AGAINST MANY SCHOOLS.

AND...

...THAT MEANS WE'D BETTER CONTINUE TO WIN!

THEREFORE...

EVERY WALL YOU SMACK INTO...

EVERY DIFFICULTY THAT HURTS YOU...

...WILL ONLY MAKE YOU STRONGER.

PHANTOM SERIES
No. 2
STAGE.46
PHANTOM SKETCH (THE FIRST PROCESS OF DRAFTING THE PICTURE AFTER THE STORY IS FORMED IN MY MIND)
CRYING RYOICHI
NONETHELESS, RYOICHI IS THE ONLY CHARACTER WHERE THERE'S A CLEAR DIVISION BETWEEN THOSE WHO LIKE HIM AND THOSE WHO DON'T.
SO, THIS ONE'S THE SKETCH THAT'S BEING OKAYED. AFTER IT WAS FURTHER REVISED, IT EVENTUALLY TOOK THE FORM PRINTED IN THE MAGAZINE.
OH. WELL, I MUST GO ON. YOU DO TOO, RYOICHI!
SHOCKED RYOICHI.
お前
ずるいよ!

STAGE.47 To that Sky (BE THERE)

JOSUI JUNIOR
AS OF TODAY, THE RETREAT IS OVER.
I THINK THE REASON YOU WON THE PRACTICE GAME IS...
...BECAUSE YOU WERE ABLE TO UNDER-STAND THE HOMEWORK YOU WERE GIVEN.

IN TWO WEEKS THE DISTRICT PRIMARY BEGINS.
I WANT YOU TO REMEMBER HOW YOU PLAYED TODAY. DO THE BEST YOU CAN.

WHEN YOU GET HOME, SLEEP WELL.
NOW, GO.
THANK YOU VERY MUCH!
YOU'VE EARNED YOUR REST.
SHŌ.

LET'S KICK SOME BALLS AT THE RIVER-BED.
THE PRACTICE MATCH WASN'T ENOUGH, WAS IT?
I'M SORRY.
BUT I'M BUSHED. I'M GOING HOME.
SEE YOU TOMORROW?
TIRED!? YOU?
UNUSUAL.
...
RYOICHI TENJO...

IT MAKES ME WORRIED.
I THOUGHT HE WAS INCREDIBLE.
BUT I WAS SCARED. HE SHOCKED ME.
YOU MAKE ME WANT TO VOMIT!
I'LL DESTROY YOU, JOSUI.
国部二
BESIDES ...
IT WAS THE FIRST TIME ANYONE EVER TALKED LIKE THAT TO ME.
BAM
...THAT POWER.
HE HAS THE ABILITY TO REALIZE HIS DREAM.
I WONDER IF EVERYONE WHO BECOMES A PROFESSIONAL PLAYER HAS THAT INTENSE POWER AND PERSONALITY?
AMONG THE THOUSANDS OF PEOPLE WHO WORK TO BECOME A PROFESSIONAL ...
...WHERE DO I FIT IN?
BECAUSE I LOVE SOCCER, I CAN'T LET YOU BEAT ME.
IF I NEED TO HAVE YOUR SKILLS TO BE A PROFESSIONAL, THEN I'LL GET THEM.
NO MATTER HOW LONG IT TAKES.
JOS

TYPE A IS SCARY WHEN HE TAKES A DEFIANT ATTITUDE.
BUT, TYPE A ALWAYS REGRETS AFTER HE SPEAKS.
WILL I EVER BE GOOD ENOUGH?
THE NEXT THING I KNEW, I WAS PICKING A FIGHT.
AM I FEAR-LESS OR WHAT?
I'M HOME.
YO.
WELCOME HOME.
AND ...
...LONG TIME NO SEE.
YOU'RE GOING TO WORK SO LATE?
BUT THIS IS SUNDAY!
I'M GOING ON A DATE.
BY THE WAY, HOW WAS THE RETREAT? DIDN'T YOU HAVE A PRACTICE MATCH TODAY?
AH, YEAH.

WE WON.
THREE TO TWO.
...HUMM.
THERE'S THIS INCREDIBLE GUY IN THE OPPOSING TEAM. ALTHOUGH HE'S MY AGE...
HE'S GOT THIS GREAT BODY AND TECHNIQUE.
HE BROKE THROUGH EVEN WHEN THREE DFs TRIED TO BLOCK HIM. HE CAN SEND THESE EXPLOSIVE BULLET SHOTS, AND YET, HE'S ACCURATE...
HE DOES SOUND PRETTY INCREDIBLE.
YOU THINK? I'M STILL SHOCKED WE WON.

THE THING IS, I'M SURE WE'RE GOING TO FACE A LOT OF OTHERS LIKE HIM WHEN WE PARTICIPATE IN THE TOKYO-WIDE CHAMPIONSHIP, OR IN THE NATIONAL CHAMPIONSHIP.
I WONDER HOW MUCH LONGER IT'S GOING TO BE BEFORE I MASTER THOSE TECHNIQUES?

SHŌ?
SORRY, BRO KŌ. YOU WERE ABOUT TO LEAVE. DON'T BE LATE.
SHŌ...
HMMM
SEE YOU LATER.
YEAH.
BEEP BEEP

SLAM
HELLO, IT'S ME. IT'S BEEN A WHILE.
IT'S ABOUT SHŌ...YES. ..I WANTED TO CALL YOU...
SLIIIDD
A PRO, HUH...
SHŌ.
TAP TAP
WHAT?
AS YOUR BROTHER, I HAVE THE GREATEST FAVOR OF MY LIFE TO ASK YOU.
HUH?
SLIIID
LET'S GO AND EAT SOMETHING YUMMY!
HUH!?

THAT'S ...THE GREATEST FAVOR OF YOUR LIFE?
YEAH. WE HAVEN'T TALKED MUCH LATELY, AND I WANTED TO SPEND SOME TIME WITH YOU.
WHAT ABOUT YOUR DATE?
AH, THANKS FOR REMINDING ME.
AH...MADAM? IT'S ME... YES...WELL, I'M NOT... FEELING WELL...PROBABLY SICK....I'M SO SORRY... BUT I CAN'T...THANK YOU. ANOTHER TIME.
KAFF SNIFFF KAF KAF
OK
WHAT ...?
YOU LIED ABOUT BEING SICK!
ONLY A LITTLE LIE.
BUT STILL ...
GRRUMMBLE
IT'S DECIDED THEN.
HEH
YAMAMOTO
THIS PLACE ?
VROOOOOO
OH, YOU MADE IT!

I'VE BEEN WAITING FOR YOU. COME IN!
TEACHER! YAMAMOTO...
I APOLOGIZE FOR BARGING IN ON SUCH SHORT NOTICE.
NO PROBLEM AT ALL. NO PROBLEM. SINCE YOUR PARENTS MOVED TO KYUSHU, YOU PROBABLY DON'T GET TO EAT ANYTHING THAT REQUIRES PREPARATION.
LET'S HAVE A DRINK, KŌ.
CAN'T. I'M DRIVING.
HOW SAD! I HAD HOPED TO SHARE A DRINK AFTER SO LONG.
PLEASE ENJOY TO YOUR HEART'S CONTENT.
YES.
BOTH MY BRO KŌ AND I...
IT'S OKAY. YOU HAVE SOME. I BROUGHT MY SPECIAL RESERVE.
...HAD HIM AS OUR TEACHER WHEN WE WERE IN ELEMENTARY SCHOOL.
YOU TALKED ME INTO IT.
HMMM, DELICIOUS!
HE'S STRICT AND EXTREMELY SCARY WHEN HE'S ANGRY...
MR. YAMAMOTO WAS THE ONLY ONE WHO SERIOUSLY LISTENED TO ME...
...WHEN I EXPRESSED MY DESIRE TO ENTER MUSASHINOMORI.
BUT HE WOULD ALWAYS LISTEN TO HIS STUDENTS' CONCERNS.
HE WAS MY FAVORITE TEACHER.
IT'S BEEN A WHILE SINCE GRADUATION. SHŌ, HAVE YOU GOTTEN TALLER?
HOW'S THE SCHOOL?
AND YET...
SIR...

I ENDED UP LEAVING MUSASHI-NOMORI.
I'M SO SORRY.

ISN'T IT YOUR DREAM TO BECOME A SOCCER PLAYER?
YES.
FOOSH
DO NOT LET YOUR GOAL BECOME YOUR OBJECTIVE.
?

IT'S NOT ABOUT *HOW YOU CAN BECOME ONE,* BUT...
...WHY YOU WANT TO BECOME ONE.

WHEN YOU BEGIN TO LOSE SIGHT, SHŌ...
...TRACE BACK THE PATH YOU TOOK, AND REMEMBER HOW YOU FIRST FELT.

WHY DID YOU ASPIRE TO BECOME A PRO, AND WHAT DID YOU WANT TO DO ONCE YOU BECOME ONE?
RUSSTLE
ALWAYS REMEMBER THAT.

ONLY THE PERSON WHO CONTINUES TO KEEP HIS INITIAL RESOLUTION CAN BECOME...
...WHO HE WANTS TO BE.
RELENT-LESSLY ...
IF YOU LIKE SOCCER ...
... PURSUE IT EARNESTLY AND STRONGLY.
THEN YOU CAN DO IT, SHŌ KAZA-MATSURI.
YES!
IS THAT RIGHT?
THAT'S WHY I WANT TO BECOME A BETTER PLAYER ...
... THAN ANYONE ELSE.

SNORRRR
HUSBAND...
YOU'RE SO HOPE-LESS.
LET HIM SLEEP. WE'RE FINE.
THANK YOU FOR THE WONDER-FUL MEAL.
COME VISIT US AGAIN.
THANK YOU VERY MUCH. PLEASE GIVE MR. YAMAMOTO OUR BEST.
SNAP
SNORKK.
THEY'RE ABOUT TO LEAVE--SHOULDN'T YOU SEE THEM OFF?
NOW YOU'RE AWAKE?
WHERE ARE THEY?
THEY LEFT.
JUST NOW.
IS THAT SO?
SKRTCH
WHAT NICE KIDS. QUITE RARE THESE DAYS.
SUCH GENTLE SOULS.
IT'S BEEN A WHILE SINCE I FELT SO GOOD ABOUT BEING A TEACHER.
SLAM
THANKS, BRO KŌ.
I REMEMBERED YOU SOUNDED THAT WAY BEFORE. WHEN YOU FIRST MET MIZUNO.
YOU'RE EASY TO READ.
I DIDN'T MEAN TO GET SO DEPRESSED, BUT...
GUESS I WAS RIGHT TO BRING YOU.
GEEZ.
DO YOU MIND HELPING ME ONCE MORE? THERE'S A PLACE I NEED TO GO.
NO PROBLEM. I'M YOUR CHAUFFEUR FOR THE DAY.
VAROOOOOOMMMM

TERAO ELEMENTARY SCHOOL

MY WONDERFUL OLD SCHOOL ...

DID THE COLOR OF THE SCHOOL BUILDING CHANGE?

THEY REPAINTED IT WHEN I WAS IN THE SIXTH GRADE.

AH.

A BALL.

TOSS

I FIRST PLAYED...

... SOCCER HERE.

EVEN THEN...

...I WAS THE SMALLEST.

I THOUGHT THE BIGGER KIDS LOOKED SO INCREDIBLY COOL COMPARED TO ME.

I HATED BEING SO SMALL.

I WATCHED THE GAME FOREVER SO I KNEW HOW TO PLAY.
BUT, THERE'S A BIG DIFFERENCE IN KNOWING IT AND ACTUALLY DOING IT. I WASN'T GOOD.
YOU WON'T BE ABLE TO PASS BY ME. WHY DON'T YOU GIVE UP!?
NO, I WON'T!
YOU --
MR. YAMA-MOTO GOT ME THIS CHANCE ...
I WON'T QUIT.
SKRUPPDD

I DON'T REMEMBER HOW I...
...PASSED BY HIM.
I WAS SO IN MY OWN HEAD...
...THE MOMENT I NEEDED TO PASS...
...THE SPACE OPENED UP IN FRONT OF ME.
SUDDENLY, THE SKY EMBRACED ME.

I LOVED THAT MOMENT.
I WANTED TO FEEL IT AGAIN.
AND I WANTED TO CONTINUE TO FEEL THAT WAY.
THAT'S WHY I KEPT PLAYING SOCCER.
I SAW THAT EXPANSE OF SKY WHEN I PASSED TATSUYA, TOO.
I REMEMBER THAT NOW!
IS THAT SO?
AND ALL AROUND ME...
...THERE ARE PEOPLE WHO SUPPORT ME.
ALL OF THEM SHARE THEIR STRENGTH WITH ME.
THAT'S WHY I STILL PERSIST.
HEY! WHO'S ENTERING THE SCHOOL AT NIGHT? YOU PLOTTING SOMETHING BAD?
OOPS, TROUBLE. RUN! SHŌ!
WAIT A SEC, BRO KŌ!

Question Corner

IT'S BEEN A WHILE SINCE I LAST HAD A QUESTION CORNER. I'LL TRY TO ANSWER ALL THE QUESTIONS MAILED ME, BUT THE FACT IS THERE WERE SO MANY THAT ARE DIFFICULT TO ANSWER. ANYHOW, LET ME TRY.

Q1: ACCORDING TO THE PROFILE, SHIGEKI APPEARS TO BE ONE YEAR OLDER THAN SHŌ AND TATSUYA. WAS THAT A MISTAKE? OR, WAS HE NOT ALLOWED TO PROCEED TO THE HIGHER GRADE? I THOUGHT THAT WAS NOT SUPPOSED TO HAPPEN IN JUNIOR HIGH SCHOOLS.

A1: IT ISN'T A MISTAKE. SHIGEKI IS ONE YEAR OLDER THAN SHŌ. IN FACT, THERE WAS A FRIEND OF MY FRIEND WHO WAS IN THE SAME GRADE DESPITE BEING OLDER. TO BE HONEST, THE REASON WHY SHIGEKI IS THERE IS A SECRET. IT'S A SECRET I WILL USE WHEN SHIGEKI IS FEATURED IN THE STORY. IF I EXPLAINED IT TO YOU NOW, IT WON'T BE EXCITING LATER, DON'T YOU THINK? IF YOU LOVE SHIGEKI, LET'S WAIT UNTIL HE HIMSELF TELLS YOU HIS STORY, OKAY? ♡

Q2: HIGUCHI, ARE YOU A MAN OR A WOMAN? I CAN'T SLEEP AT NIGHT THINKING ABOUT IT, SO PLEASE TELL ME.

A2: IT'S A PROBLEM IF YOU CAN'T FALL ASLEEP AT NIGHT. AS FAR AS I'M CONCERNED, I THINK KNOWING MY SEX DOESN'T MATTER...LIKE THE CROW SHERLOCK HOLMES IS SAYING, THE CLUE IS RIGHT IN FRONT OF YOU. HAVE YOU READ THE MANGA WELL? THERE ARE CLUES HIDDEN ALL OVER THEM.

YOU ALREADY KNOW THE PERPETRATOR... I MEAN, THE SEX OF HIGUCHI!

WELL, MY ANSWERS DON'T QUITE MAKE IT AS ANSWERS, I SUPPOSE, BUT SINCE THERE ISN'T ENOUGH SPACE LEFT, THIS IS ALL I CAN DO FOR NOW.

STAGE.48 During the 88 Minutes

... HEY.

WHY ARE THERE SO MANY OLD GEEZERS HERE?

APPARENTLY, IT'S SOME-THING TO DO WITH THE SOCCER TEAM.

STAGE.48
During the 88 Minutes
...HERE ARE THE MEMBERS OF AKASHIA SOCCER ASSOCIATION WHO WILL PLAY A MINI-GAME WITH YOU.
AKASHIA
AKASHIA

THEY'RE ALL EXCELLENT PLAYERS WHO USED TO TAKE ACTIVE PARTS IN THE EMPEROR'S CUPS AND SUCH. YOU CAN LEARN FROM THEM.

TAAA-WHEEET
TAP
TAP
TAP
I'M NOT HOLDING BACK JUST 'CAUSE THEY'RE OLD.
YO!
WOOOSHH
HERE!
TOKU-JIROU.
WHOOMP
AH.
KRAKKK

WHERE WILL HE KICK?

AH.

HE'S GONE !?

BOMP

BOMP

BOMP

WHOA! MY BACK!
HEH
WHIII
JUST KID-DING.
HUHHH
HUNH?
HUH?
AKASHIA
WHIIP
WHOOOMBLE
POMP
POMP
HUHHH?
WE DID IT! FIRST POINT.
NO WAY. IMPOSSIBLE.

BAMMMM
YAHHHH!
WHAPP
KAKU, IT'S NOT OKAY FOR A GK TO RUN AWAY.
HEH HEH
WELL, I'D BE DEAD IF IT HIT ME, AND I'VE ALREADY DECIDED I'M GONNA DIE ON A TATAMI MAT!
NOT GOOD ...
THEY MAKE ME PLAY ALL WRONG.
IF I STAY CLOSE, THE BALL COMES OVER.
MAKES IT EASY FOR ME.
HAH
AKASHIA
WHOOMP

GEEZ. HOW COULD KIDS FOUL UP SO MUCH AGAINST THE OLD GEEZERS!?
MAYBE YOU SHOULD GET OUT THERE, SANTA?
ARE YOU JOKING?
FINALLY IT'S LORD SANTA YAMAGUCHI'S TURN.
HEE HEE HEE
MAMORU, SANTA WILL TAKE YOUR SPOT.
HEE HEE HEE
ONCE I'M IN ...
YOU'RE NOT GETTING AHEAD NOW.
EEYYAAHHHHH
WHOOSHHH
DON'T UNDER-ESTIMATE ME, PUP.
HUH...
!

WHHO-
OOMMM
YAHHHH!
GASP.
POIT
WHY ARE THEY DIFFERENT FROM US?
TECHNIQUE?
EVEN THOUGH WE'RE STRONGER AND FASTER, THE OLD MEN ARE CONTROLLING THE BALL.
NO. I HAVE A FEELING IT'S NOT ABOUT PLAY OR THEIR TECHNIQUE...
GOT-CHA!
FWOOP
ARRRGH!
BOOM
DIRTY TRICK!
TAKING AN ENEMY BY SURPRISE ...
HEH HEH
...IS AN ACCEPT-ABLE STRATEGY.
DON'T GET UPSET.
TAP TAP

HOW COME WE LET THEM SCORE FIVE POINTS?

IT MUST BE GREAT TO BE ABLE TO USE ALL YOUR STRENGTH.

BECAUSE WE DON'T HAVE MUCH STAMINA, WE'VE GOT TO USE OUR MINDS.

READ THIS WAY

TROUBLED BECAUSE YOU HAVE TO PLAY AGAINST THE GRANDPAS?
SNORT.
I CAN'T BE SERIOUS PLAYING AGAINST OLD MEN.

REALLY? YOU LOOKED PRETTY SERIOUS WHEN YOU WERE AT IT.
HA HA HA

I BET BEFORE THIS MINI-GAME STARTED, YOU WERE SURE YOU'D WIN 10 TO 0, RIGHT?
YOU'RE IN BETTER SHAPE, SO HOW WERE THEY ABLE TO TAKE FIVE POINTS?

THE ANSWER TO THAT QUESTION IS THE KEY TO HOW YOU BECOME STRONGER.
THE KEY TO BECOMING STRONGER?

LET ME GIVE YOU A HINT.
YOU ALL KNOW OF MARADONA, RIGHT?
YES.
DIEGO MARADONA
THE WORLD'S BEST PLAYER, WHO, IN THE 1986 MEXICO CHAMPIONSHIP, PERFORMED THAT LEGENDARY "PASSING FIVE." DESPITE HIS 5'4" STATURE, HE CHARMED HIS FANS BY PASSING GIGANTIC DFs ONE AFTER ANOTHER. HIS ABILITY TO BREAK THROUGH AT THE CRITICAL MOMENT, HIS ELEGANT STYLE OF DRIBBLING, HIS PASS THAT TAKES OTHERS BY SURPRISE --ALL OF THESE ARE DONE WITH A WILD FLARE. HE'S BEEN CALLED THE VERY LAST SUPERSTAR OF THE CENTURY. AS A REPRESENTATIVE PLAYER OF THE ARGENTINEANS, HE WON THE WORLD CUP ONCE AND WAS THE RUNNER-UP ONCE.

THERE'S NO COMPARISON BETWEEN THE GRANDPAS AND MARADONA IN TERMS OF THE AMOUNT OF VIGOR OR THE TECHNIQUE, BUT AS A MATTER OF FACT, THERE IS ONE THING THAT'S COMMON.
HOW MANY TOTAL MINUTES DURING THE 90-MINUTE GAME DOES MARADONA, AS THE GOAL GETTER, HAVE THE BALL?
WHAT?
WELL, LET ME THINK.
SINCE HE'S SO INVOLVED WITH SCORING, HOW ABOUT 20 MINUTES?
THE ANSWER IS ABOUT TWO MINUTES.
HUH? NO WAY.
SUCCESSFUL PLAYERS ARE CHECKED BY THE OPPONENTS. THAT SHORTENS THE TIME THEY HAVE THE BALL.
ONLY TWO MINUTES DURING THE 90-MINUTE GAME!?
THAT'S RIGHT. WITH THOSE TWO MINUTES ALONE, HE BECAME THE WORLD SUPERSTAR.
THE GRANDPAS, WHO DON'T HAVE YOUR STAMINA, TOOK FIVE POINTS FROM YOU...
WHAT DOES THAT MEAN TO SCORE? THE ANSWER IS RIGHT IN THERE.

WHY CAN'T THE COACH JUST TELL US?

IF YOU ONLY WANT TO BE TOLD EVERYTHING, YOUR BRAIN WON'T GROW.

GEEZ.

AFTER ALL, THEY'RE STILL UTILIZING THEIR BODIES ONLY.

I BET THE CHILDREN ARE THINKING IT WAS NOT SUPPOSED TO BE LIKE THIS.

EXCUUSE ME!

WHOOOMBLE

WHIII

HUHHH

HUNH?

HEH

AH.

HERE!

YO!

...HOW COULD THEY EASILY SCORE FIVE POINTS? OUR DEFENDERS WERE DOING THEIR BEST.

POMP

POMP

I UNDERSTAND HOW WE COULD EASILY SCORE FIVE POINTS SINCE WE HAVE THE ADVANTAGE OF STAMINA, BUT...

BECAUSE WE DON'T HAVE MUCH STAMINA, WE'VE GOT TO USE OUR BRAINS.

THAT'S GOT TO BE PART OF IT.

BUT I DON'T THINK THE ISSUE IS ONLY ABOUT TECHNIQUE.

THEY DON'T MOVE MUCH. INSTEAD THEY PASS ACCURATELY AND QUICKLY, RELAYING THE BALL.

THEY'RE REALLY GOOD AT LETTING GO OF THEIR BALL.

AND SINCE THE AMOUNT OF TIME ANY ONE OF THEM HAS THE BALL IS SO SHORT -- IT'S HARD FOR THE DFs TO MARK THEM.

YOU KNOW, INSTEAD OF JUST THINKING ABOUT IT, IT WOULD BE BETTER TO PRACTICE.

HIDEOMI! TATSUYA.

LEND ME A HAND.

IN THE FIRST HALF, THE FW GRANDPA SHOT AFTER HE FREED HIMSELF FROM HIDEOMI.

HIDEOMI WAS ALREADY MARKING THE GRAND-PA.

AND HE ...

WHOOOOSH

...UN-MARKED HIMSELF ...

HE DIDN'T MOVE THAT MUCH.

NOT AT ALL. I THINK HE FREED HIMSELF PRETTY EASILY.

REALLY?

YOU DON'T GET IT, DO YOU?

THOOM

DIRTY TRICKS?
THE REASON THOSE GEEZERS SCORED FIVE POINTS IS THAT THEY USED DIRTY TRICKS.
DON'T YOU GET IT?
I MEAN, HIS DENTURES. HIS DENTURES!
I GUESS IT'S NOT THE HAND BUT THE TEETH.
HE DROPPED THEM, AND I WAS TOTALLY TAKEN BY SURPRISE, AND... ER...
...WILL YOU LISTEN TO WHAT I'M SAYING?
THAT'S WHY...
YEP. THEY'VE GOT THIS KNACK FOR DOING IT.
THAT GEEZER! WHILE I WAS DISTRACTED BY HIS DENTURES, HE ESCAPED... I MEAN, HE PASSED ME!!
HMMM.
WHERE WILL HE KICK?
AH.
WHILE BEING DISTRACTED ...PASSED BY...
HE'S GONE!?
AH!
HIDEOMI AND TATSUYA, ONCE MORE.
I GOT IT.
KNOCK IT OFF.
I WAS IN THE MIDDLE OF EXPLAINING...
THANKS, SANTA!
?
NO PROB. LONG AS YOU GOT IT.
LET'S START THE SECOND HALF!
TAAAAI-WHEEETT!

SKUK
SKUK
THE BEST WAY TO SCORE IS TO CONTROL THE BALL WHEN I'M BOTH FREE AND FACING FORWARD.
BUT, IN REALITY, WHEN I'M MARKED THIS HARD, I CAN'T EASILY FACE FORWARD.
THAT MEANS, I MUST BREAK AWAY FROM THE DF.
SO WHEN DID THE GRANDPA, WHO DIDN'T SEEM LIKE HE WAS GOING TO BREAK FROM THE MARK...
...MAKE HIS MOVE?

SKRIIIIKK

NO MATTER HOW...

...SEVERE THE MARK IS...

THAT'S WHEN HIS EYES FOLLOW WHERE THE BALL'S HEADED.
AKASHIA
AT THAT MOMENT ...
...I VANISH FROM THE DF's SIGHT.
AKASHIA
AKASHIA

THE BATTLE STARTS NOT AFTER BUT BEFORE I GET THE BALL!!
WHOOOMP
YOU'RE RIGHT, SHŌ.
ONLY THOSE WHO CONTINUE TO THINK ABOUT HOW TO VANISH FROM THE SIGHT OF THE DEFENDERS CAN...
HAH!
...SEIZE THE GLORY OF THOSE TWO MINUTES!!
THAT KID.
HE'S STILL ROUGH, BUT HE USES HIS HEAD.

STAGE.49 Quickening!

IN 1998 THE TAMA DISTRICT, INCLUDING JOSUI, DIVIDED INTO 8 BLOCKS. EXCEPT FOR THE TOP 4 OF THE PREVIOUS CHAMPIONSHIP, THE WINNER AND THE 2ND THROUGH 5TH OF EACH DISTRICT (CONSIDERED THE TOP TIER SCHOOLS OF THE TAMA REPRESENTATIVE DETERMINATION GAME) MAY PLAY IN THE TOKYO CHAMPIONSHIP.

OUR GOAL IS THE NATIONAL CHAMPION-SHIP!
THIS YEAR, WE MUST AIM TO BE NUMBER ONE.
CHATTER
CHATTER
CAPTAIN KATSURŌ.
I WONDER IF THEY'LL WIN THEIR WAY UP.
OF COURSE THEY WILL, SEIJI.
THEY'RE NOT THE KIND OF TEAM THAT WILL BE STOPPED AT THE DISTRICT PRIMARY.
BESIDES...
YOU MEAN JOSUI?
...SINCE I'M A 9TH GRADER, THIS IS MY LAST CHANCE TO PLAY SOCCER AS A JUNIOR HIGH STUDENT.
I WANT TO PLAY AGAINST THEM ONE MORE TIME.

STAGE.49 Quickening!

JOSUI JUNIOR HIGH S
HMMMM
SO WHERE'S THE SOCCER TEAM?
CAN'T FIND THEM ANY-WHERE.
!
AAHHHHHH

World Soccer
Incredible Players
GK Gr
Worl
You can become Gilmar too!
BAMMM
WHOOSH
Watch out!
This is...
..the punching!
SLAPP

NOT QUITE, MAYBE?
WHOOM
WORLD
CAN BECOME GILMAR TOO!
YOU'RE ...
...THE JOSUI'S GK?
YEAH.
HMMM, SO THERE'S BEEN A CHANGE.
PONK
THAT MEANS THAT BLONDE MUST'VE BECOME A FW...
YUP! THAT MAKES IT FUN. ♡
WHO ARE YOU?
YOU'RE NOT FROM OUR SCHOOL.

SEIJI FUJI-SHIRO!
I'M DAICHI FUWA.
DON'T YOU KNOW ME?
YOU'RE SEIJI FUJI-SHIRO. YOU JUST TOLD ME.
THAT'S NOT WHAT I MEANT ...
SO?
WHERE ARE THE OTHERS?
THEY'LL BE HERE SOON.
IT'S PROBABLY THEIR TURN TO CLEAN CLASSROOMS OR SOMETHING.
SO WHY DON'T WE HAVE SOME FUN UNTIL THEY SHOW UP?
YOU KNOW I'M A STRIKER.
BASED ON THAT LAST KICK, YOU WON'T PASS ME.
WHAMP

HMM?
WHOEVER THEY ARE, THEY'RE PRACTICING.
SEEMS SO.
WHAM
DAICHI AND...
... THE OTHER GUY IS ...
!
WHOOMP

SEIJI!
WHY IS SEIJI OF MUSA-SHINOMORI HERE?
HEY, LOOK AT DAICHI.
HE'S SAVING EVERY SHOT ...
... MADE BY SEIJI.
THOOMP
PRETTY GOOD.

YO. LONG TIME NO SEE!
HELLO.
YOU'VE CHANGED YOUR GK.
THE NEW GUY'S GOOD.
YOU'RE AN ENEMY. WHY ARE YOU HERE? TO SPY!?
IDIOT.
HOW EMBARRASSING.
WAP
OUCH!
NO ONE'S GONNA SPY ON US.
COURSE I AM.
YOU'RE JOKING, RIGHT?
NO WAY.
HUH?
YOU REALLY SHOULDN'T THINK OF YOURSELF AS INFERIOR.
SINCE I WAS COMING HERE TO SPY, I THOUGHT I'D BRING ...
WHISHH
... THIS.
WHAT?
SWISHH
A GIFT FOR THE GUYS AT THE FRONT-LINE. ♡
WHAT IS IT?
WHAT DID HE BRING?
IT'S A BAG OF SNACKS ...
MY FAVORITE'S THE KIMCHEE-FLAVORED PORK...
SEIJI OF MUSA-SHINOMORI. YOU MEAN THAT STRIKER ...?
HE WAS SELECTED AMONG THAT JUNIOR ....

SINCE WE'RE EXCUSED FROM THE PRIMARIES...

...I WANT THE JOSUI TEAM...

...TO WIN EVERY GAME 'TIL YOU MAKE IT TO THE TOKYO CHAMPIONSHIP.

OTHERWISE IT WON'T BE FUN FOR US.

PROMISE YOU'LL MAKE IT TO THE SUMMER CHAMPIONSHIP.

HE'S ENCOURAGING US...

...HE WANTS US TO WIN...

...SO THAT WE CAN HAVE A REMATCH.

WE WON'T LOSE...

UNTIL WE GET TO PLAY AGAINST MUSASHINOMORI.

YEP!

YOU SURE? I BEG YOU! THE CAPTAIN AND I WERE TELLING EVERYONE TO WATCH OUT FOR JOSUI DURING THE SUMMER CHAMPIONSHIP, BUT...

...THEY LAUGH AT US!

IT'S REALLY MORTIFYING!

S -- SEIJI?

WHAT'S THIS RACKET ABOUT?

AH, COACH MATSUSHITA.

SOUJŪ?

AH.

ARE YOU THE ...

...SOUJŪ MATSUSHITA, THE FORMER CAPTAIN OF BOTH SHINKAWA DENKO AND JAPAN REPRESENTATIVE TEAM?

YEAH?

I'M A HUGE FAN OF YOURS!

I CAN'T BELIEVE I'D MEET YOU HERE.

THIS IS SO EXCITING.

MY DAD AND BROTHER ARE ALSO HUGE FANS OF YOURS. I'M SO GONNA BRAG ABOUT THIS. ♡

YOU'RE SO YOUNG. HOW DO YOU KNOW ABOUT ME?

I WATCHED THE DIAMOND SOCCER VIDEO!

S-- SEIJI'S ...

... A FAN, JUST LIKE US.

ROAAARRRR

I DON'T KNOW WHY YOU BECAME JOSUI'S COACH, BUT...
...IF SOUJŪ MATSUSHITA IS THE COACH, WE'D BETTER WATCH OUT.
YOU WANT TO PLAY WITH THEM,
DO YOU, LAD?
YOU BET.
PLEASE.
ARE YOU SERIOUS?
IS THAT OKAY?
YOUR COACH ALREADY SAID YES. ♡
COACH!

ARE YOU SURE? YOU FORGET HE'S OUR ENEMY TEAM'S ACE PLAYER.

WE DON'T HAVE ANY SECRETS.

THIS WILL BE FINE.
BESIDES...
AND, THAT APPLIES TO THEM, TOO.

HIS MOVEMENTS ARE PERFECT...

...AND ACCURATE.

HE DRIBBLES LIKE THE BALL STICKS TO HIM.

SHŌ.

WHOOM

BAM
OW!
IS THIS A KICK-BASE?
SORRY.
DON'T SWEAT IT!
Y'KNOW, JOSUI IS A GOOD TEAM.

YEAH.
EVERY-ONE LOVES THE GAME AND TRIES THEIR BEST. AND WE CAN ALWAYS RELY ON TATSUYA AND SHIGEKI.

WHAT?
I'VE PLAYED AGAINST JOSUI. I KNOW.
YEAH, TATSUYA AND SHIGEKI ARE GOOD PLAYERS, BUT THE STRENGTH THAT MOVES THE TEAM... THE CENTER OF THE TEAM...

WHAT'RE YOU TALKING ABOUT?
THE TEAM EXISTS BECAUSE OF YOU.

...IS YOU.

N--NO WAY. I'M STILL UNSKILLED.
IF THAT'S SO, YOU'RE EVEN MORE IMPORTANT. WITH YOUR PASSION ALONE, YOU CORNERED US.
IF SOMEONE LIKE YOU GAINS TECHNIQUE, ANYTHING CAN HAPPEN.

I'M NOT SURE HOW TO SAY IT, BUT I BELIEVE YOU DON'T HAVE A LIMIT.
BECAUSE THERE'S NO TOP, YOU CAN DEVELOP FOREVER ...

I THOUGHT CAPTAIN KATSURŌ WAS INCREDIBLE, BUT...
... WITH YOU I FEEL AWE.

OH WELL!
I COULD BE RIGHT OR WRONG, BUT IT'S WHAT I BELIEVE.

SOME-HOW, HE'S TOTALLY ASSIMILATED, DON'T YOU THINK?
THAT ONE! THE EXTREMELY RARE CHOKER! I'M SO JEALOUS.
TO KNOW THE VALUE OF THIS THING, YOU ARE AN EXPERT TOO.
I MEAN, HIM...
HE'S THE KIND OF GUY YOU CAN'T GET ANGRY AT.
I LIKE JOSUI MORE THAN MY SCHOOL. IT'S A LOT OF FUN.
EVER THINK OF TRANSFER-RING?
DING DING
IF ONLY I COULD ...
DING DING
OOPS, I'M IN TROUBLE.
I'M SUPPOSED TO BE AT THE HOSPITAL. I SHOULD GET BACK.
SEE YA.
SEIJI.
IT'S GOOD HERE, BUT I BELONG TO MUSA-SHINO-MORI.
'SIDES, UNLESS I'M YOUR ENEMY, I WON'T BE ABLE TO PLAY AGAINST YOU.
HEY, DAICHI!

ONE MATCH LEFT, THE VERY LAST ONE!
GRRRR
BAM
MMMMMM!

SPOING
HUH!
WHOOSH

WHOOMP
DOES THIS...
...MEAN HE WASN'T PLAYING SERIOUSLY BEFORE...?
IF YOU'RE A GK, YOU'D BETTER REMEMBER SEIJI FUJISHIRO, THE NO. 9 OF MUSASHI-NOMORI.
SHŌ!
REMEMBER. YOU HAVE TO WIN.

I'LL BE WAITING FOR YOU, JOSUI.

WOW. WHAT A GUY.

YEAH. AND HE NOTICED ...

... ME.

I WANT TO PLEASE HIM!

SO IF WE WANT TO HAVE A RE-MATCH AGAINST MUSASHINOMORI WE NEED TO KEEP WINNING.

TO BATTLE OUR WAY THROUGH, I'LL NEED A WEAPON...

...THAT EVEN SEIJI AND KATSURŌ CAN'T STOP.

A WEAPON THAT'S ALL MINE.

THANKS TO YOU.
One Year Anniversary.
CONGRATS
WHISTLE!
AND THANK YOU FOR THE SECOND YEAR. ♡

A WEAPON THAT'S ALL MINE.
SO IF WE WANT TO HAVE A RE-MATCH AGAINST MUSASHINOMORI WE NEED TO KEEP WINNING.
STAGE.50 Weapon Of My Own
MY JOB IS TO JUMP INTO THE SPACE AND SHOOT...
FOOOOSHH
BUT THAT'S NOT ENOUGH.
BAM
SOME-THING THAT CAN BREAK THE OPPONENTS' FORMATION WHEN THEIR DEFENSE IS STRONG.

WHAT I NOW NEED THE MOST IS...!
...THE ABILITY TO DRIBBLE!
FWISHHHH
STAGE.50
Weapon Of My Own

KLIK
FWISHHH

THAT'S THREE SECONDS OFF MY BEGINNING.

I CAN GO AROUND WITH THE BALL WITH-OUT KNOCKING THEM OFF NOW, BUT ...
...I WONDER IF THIS TRAINING IS ENOUGH.

WHO OSH
!
EVEN IF YOU DO WELL AGAINST A STATIONARY OPPONENT ...
...HOW WILL YOU DO AGAINST A MOVING OPPONENT?

CAPTAIN HONMA!

YOU MEAN, EX-CAPTAIN.

HAVEN'T SEEN YOU SINCE I LOST AGAINST YOU.

A GAME FOR THE POSITION OF CAPTAIN.

OUR TEAM WILL BE STRONGER IF I BECOME THE CAPTAIN INSTEAD OF YOU.

IN FACT, THE WINNER SHOULD ALWAYS BE CAPTAIN, FROM

LET'S NOT DO IT, CAPTAIN!

NO, I MADE A PROMISE.

TATSUYA IS NOW THE CAPTAIN.

NO, THAT'S RIDICULOUS.

I'VE HAD IT! I QUIT!

FWISHH
!
!?
PAM
LET'S PLAY.
HUH?
I'LL BE YOUR PRACTICE PARTNER.
OKAY. SO LET'S PLAY.
S-SURE.

RIGHT.

FWISHHH

WHY IS HE HELPING ME LIKE THIS?

WHOOSH

EVER SINCE I LOST...

...I'VE BEEN WATCHING YOU GUYS.

HUH?
DON'T STOP!
O-- OKAY!
EARLY ON...
THUNK
...I HATED YOU ALL.
SKROOM
I THOUGHT YOU'D NEVER AMOUNT TO ANY-THING.
YOU COULDN'T WORK IT OUT.
I WAS HOPING YOU'D GIVE UP.
NUTS!

HON-MA...

WHEN A DF LINES UP RIGHT BESIDE YOU, YOU PUSH YOUR BODY BETWEEN THE BALL AND THE DF!

...ONCE
THE GAME
STARTED...
...WHAT
I SAW...
BUT...
EVERYONE THOUGHT MUSASHI-NOMORI WOULD BEAT YOU SO BADLY...
...IS YOU GUYS, MATCHED EVENLY AGAINST...
...THE SUPER POWERFUL OPPONENT!
THAT'S WHEN I REALIZED...
IF I WERE THERE, THAT MARK COULD'VE ...
WHAT'RE YOU DOING THERE?
ARRGH!

...THAT I LOVED SOCCER AFTER ALL.
BUT I NEVER DID ANYTHING TO EXPRESS THAT LOVE.
I THOUGHT THE REASON THINGS DIDN'T WORK OUT WAS OTHER PEOPLE'S FAULT...
...THAT THEY DIDN'T RECOGNIZE MY TALENT.
BUT UNLESS YOU TRY YOUR VERY BEST...
YOU CAN'T REALLY FEEL THAT JOY.
SO I RAN AWAY...
I HAD NO RIGHT TO PLAY ANYMORE.

EVEN THOUGH YOU LOST AGAINST MUSASHI-NOMORI ...
...TO ME...
...YOU GUYS WERE INCREDIBLE.
HONMA ...
...LET'S ...PLAY ...
... AGAIN!
IF YOU ASKED THEM PROPERLY, TATSUYA AND THE REST WOULD --
SHŌ.
THANKS.
BUT I MADE THAT DECISION, AND HAVE NO INTENTION OF GOING BACK.
BUT --
THAT DOESN'T MEAN I QUIT PLAYING SOCCER!

WHEN I ENTER HIGH SCHOOL, I'LL START OVER AGAIN, JUST LIKE YOU DID.
AND THIS TIME, I WON'T MAKE THAT MISTAKE.

HONMA SEMPAI!

YOU STILL ADDRESS ME AS "SEMPAI," EH?
I HAVEN'T DONE ANY-THING TO DESERVE BEING CALLED THAT.

PAMM

FWOOM

SINCE I CAN'T DO ANYTHING ELSE FOR YOU, I'LL BECOME YOUR PRACTICE WALL!
TRY BREAKING THROUGH ME!
SHŌ !!
YES!

FOOOSHH
WHIIIIPP
BAMM
WATCH IT.
TOO SLOW! DIDN'T I TELL YOU TO VARY THE SPEED?
RIGHT!
WHIIIPP
WATCH THE OPPONENT'S MOVE CAREFULLY!
YEAH!
YOU'RE NOT HANDLING THE BALL RIGHT.
THINK OF LIFTING.
WHOOM

WHISHHHH

FOOOOM

SKROOOMM

I WON'T LET YOU!

HIS ATTENTION ...
... IS DIRECTED TO THE BALL.

THIS IS IT!
SKDOOOO

CAN WE TRY AGAIN?
HUFF WAI..T. N..NO MORE... TODAY... HUFF
TO-MORROW... SAME... TIME... OKAY...?
HUFF
HUFFF
HUFF
HUFF
OKAY ...

I'M SURPRISED.
HE'S SO MUCH BETTER THAN WHEN HE GOT HERE. IT'S LIKE HE'S A DIFFERENT PERSON.

IN ADDITION TO HIS GOOD NATURE ...

...HE DOESN'T HAVE FALSE PRIDE. MAYBE THAT'S WHY HE LEARNS SO FAST.

HE COULD BECOME...

...AN INCREDIBLE PLAYER SOMEDAY.
A FULL MOON.

WHISTLE!

STAGE.51

The Will That Shall Not Be Defeated

WHISSHHH
BUT DON'T BE SATISFIED BECAUSE YOU CAN PASS BY US.
YOU'LL BE PLAYING AGAINST MUCH BETTER DFs AT THE CHAMPION-SHIP.
YOU'RE GETTING IT.

I'LL DO MY BEST!
THANK YOU VERY MUCH...
...SEN-PAI.
SHŌ.
YES?
WILL YOU GIVE THIS TO TATSUYA FOR ME?
A NOTE-BOOK?
!
THIS IS--
IF YOU'RE GRATE-FUL, YOU'D BETTER WIN.
THAT'LL BE MY REWARD.

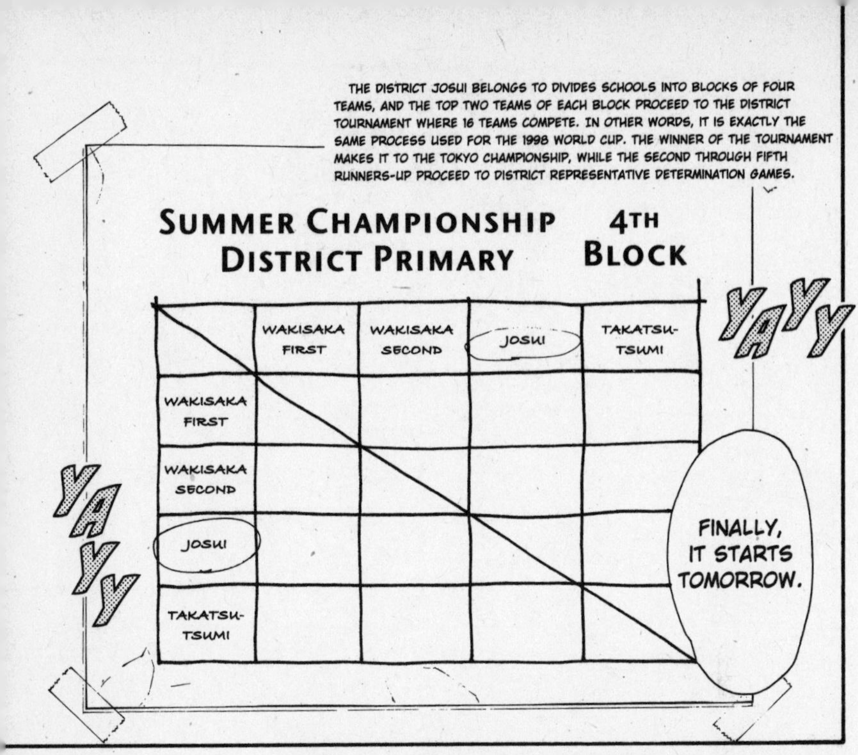

THE DISTRICT JOSUI BELONGS TO DIVIDES SCHOOLS INTO BLOCKS OF FOUR TEAMS, AND THE TOP TWO TEAMS OF EACH BLOCK PROCEED TO THE DISTRICT TOURNAMENT WHERE 16 TEAMS COMPETE. IN OTHER WORDS, IT IS EXACTLY THE SAME PROCESS USED FOR THE 1998 WORLD CUP. THE WINNER OF THE TOURNAMENT MAKES IT TO THE TOKYO CHAMPIONSHIP, WHILE THE SECOND THROUGH FIFTH RUNNERS-UP PROCEED TO DISTRICT REPRESENTATIVE DETERMINATION GAMES.

SUMMER CHAMPIONSHIP DISTRICT PRIMARY 4TH BLOCK

	WAKISAKA FIRST	WAKISAKA SECOND	JOSUI	TAKATSUTSUMI
WAKISAKA FIRST				
WAKISAKA SECOND				
JOSUI				
TAKATSUTSUMI				

YAYY

YAYY

FINALLY, IT STARTS TOMORROW.

STAGE.51 The Will That Shall Not Be Defeated

FOR US, IN SUMMER, THE DISTRICT PRIMARY STARTS WITH THE LEAGUE MATCH.

IT OVERLAPS WITH WORLD CUP IN TERMS OF TIME OF THE YEAR AS WELL AS PROCESS.

THE FIRST OPPONENT IS THE POWERFUL WAKISAKA FIRST JUNIOR HIGH. OUR SCHOOL HAS NEVER WON AGAINST THEM.

WE'VE GOT THE WORST RECORD AMONG THE TEAMS IN THIS BLOCK.

UNLESS WE BECOME THE WINNER OF THE FOURTH BLOCK, WE WON'T BE ABLE TO MAKE IT TO DISTRICT TOURNAMENT, LET ALONE THE TOKYO CHAMPIONSHIP...

WE HAVE TO DO OUR BEST!

HERE.
FROM HONMA TO CAPTAIN TATSUYA ...
FOR THE SUMMER CHAMPIONSHIP.
...
FLIPP
THE DATA ON THE OPPOSING TEAMS!?
WAKISAKA SECOND
HE WANTS YOU TO MAKE GOOD USE OF IT DURING THE SUMMER CHAMPIONSHIP.
I'M SORRY, TATSUYA.
BUT AFTER PRACTICING WITH THE TEAM, I HAD TWO OLDER STUDENTS HELP ME.
YOU KNOW, I SUSPECTED SOMETHING LIKE THAT.
WAS IT THAT OBVIOUS?
TATSUYA ...

※ A STUD IS THE SPIKE AFFIXED TO THE BOTTOM OF THE SOCCER SHOES. ONE TYPE IS PERMANENTLY AFFIXED AND ANOTHER TYPE IS REMOVABLE.

I WAS JUST SAYING WHAT I THINK YOU'RE FEELING.

OH, REALLY?

DON'T BE EMBARRASSED.

I CAN UNDERSTAND WHY THEY WANTED TO HELP.

WHEN YOU SEE HOW HARD HE TRIES, YOU WANT TO HELP HIM.

AND I KNOW HOW YOU MUST FEEL WHEN A CHILD WHO NEEDED YOUR HELP IS NOW INDEPENDENT.

BUT IT'S NOT GOOD TO BE OVER-PROTECTIVE. LET HIM GO.

TAP

EXCUSE ME ?!

I'M SURE YOU'VE ALREADY NOTICED.

HE DOESN'T REALIZE IT, BUT THESE PAST SEVERAL WEEKS HIS ABILITY HAS GOTTEN SO MUCH BETTER.

SOME-DAY HE'S GONNA BE REALLY GOOD.

IF WE DON'T WORK HARDER, HE'S GOING TO LEAVE US BEHIND.

BAKERY
GEEZ, WHY DO I HAVE TO ACCOMPANY THEM SO I CAN CARRY THE BAGS?
DID YOU SAY SOME-THING?
NOTHING.
THIS STORY TAKES PLACE RIGHT BEFORE THE 1998 WORLD CUP. (SORRY.)
THE WORLD CUP IS EVERY-WHERE.
Western Style Cakes
OFFICIAL JAPANESE REPRESENTATIVES PHOTO BOOK OF THE JAPANESE PLAYERS IS NOW AVAILABLE.
CONGRATULATIONS ON MAKING IT TO THE WORLD CUP FOR THE FIRST TIME.
Western Style Cakes
BECAUSE IN THE EVENING ON THE DAY AFTER TOMORROW IS THE JAPAN VS. ARGENTINA MATCH.
EVEN THOSE WHO DON'T WATCH J-LEAGUE BECOME OVERNIGHT SOCCER CRITICS.
I DON'T LIKE IT.
ANY-THING THAT HELPS THEM LOVE SOCCER IS GOOD.
SO LONG AS THEY DON'T LOSE THEIR INTEREST RIGHT AFTER THIS.
WHAT ARE YOU TALKING ABOUT? ONE VICTORY, ONE LOSS AND ONE TIE. THEY MADE IT THROUGH THE PRIMARY.
I CAN'T STAND THE ANTICIPATION OF AN EASY VICTORY.
PINCHHH
OW OW OUCH!

DO YOU THINK THE JAPANESE TEAM HAS NO CHANCE TO WIN?

THAT'S NOT WHAT I MEANT, BUT...

!

IT'S THE SAME WITH ME... EVEN IF WE'RE REGARDED AS WEAK, AS LONG AS WE'RE GOING TO THE DISTRICT PRIMARY, I DON'T INTEND TO LOSE.

...

THUD

DRIPP

HUMPH ...

NO! THE BOX FOR MY...

...PREDATORS!

I'M SO SORRY. LET ME FIX IT RIGHT AWAY--

NO! DON'T TOUCH.

RRIIIPP

OOPS?

NOOOOO!

CALM DOWN, CAPTAIN! YOUR SHOES ARE SAFE.

YOU FOOL. WITHOUT THE BOX, THEIR VALUE IS CUT IN HALF.

HANDKER-CHIEF.

HANDKER ...AH.

PLEASE CLEAN UP YOUR BLOODY NOSE.

DRIIIPP

ER-- PLEASE USE THIS TO WIPE --

WHIIP

GEEZ.

DAB DAB

HM?

PHEW

THUD

WOAAA, CAPTAIN!
HEH HEH
IT'S BAD. HIS EYES ARE ROLLED UP.
NUTS!
YOU OKAY, CAPTAIN?
THIS IS A BAD DAY. I'M GOING HOME... FAST.

HMM ...?

A HOT GIRL!

RUSHHH

OH, NO, CAPTAIN'S BAD HABIT ...

TAME-GOROU?
WHAT AN UGLY NAME!

NO. THERE'S A SPACE. ARAMAKITAME.
HOLD ON, CAPTAIN!
AH, THERE YOU ARE!

!
HAVE YOU PAID?

IT'S THAT BRAT!

I SEE, I SEE, I GOT IT.
THEY KNOW THEY CAN'T DEFEAT US, SO THEY'RE TRYING TO PSYCHE US OUT. BUT THAT WON'T WORK.
THE STRATEGY OF CONFUSION, HUH?

THAT GIRL... THEY'RE MEMBERS OF THE SOCCER TEAM?
JOSUI SOCCER TEAM!?

IS IT OKAY FOR SUCH WEAKLINGS TO FOOL AROUND INSTEAD OF PRACTICE?

THE GAME'S TOMORROW.
YOU ALL RELAXED?

... HUH?
THEY'RE THE WAKISAKA. WE'RE PLAYING AGAINST THEM FIRST. THAT PRETENTIOUS GUY'S THEIR CAPTAIN.
OOPS, MORE TROUBLE.
HEH

THE ONE BEHIND YOU. HE'S YOUR INFERIOR, RIGHT?
YOU'RE NOT DISCIPLINING HIM. BUT I ASSUME WITHOUT A NINTH GRADER THAT CAN'T BE HELPED.
SO WHAT ARE YOU GOING TO DO? MY BOX IS BROKEN.
SO WHAT?
YEAH, SO WHAT? I DIDN'T DO IT ON PURPOSE.
HOW DARE-- ?
LOOK. WE'RE SORRY.

LET ME APOLOGIZE FOR HIM.
BOW
!
FORGIVE HIM.
SHŌ, YOU DON'T HAVE TO APOLOGIZE.
HEH
WELL, I CAN FORGIVE HIM BUT MAKE SURE HE'S CAREFUL TOMORROW.
WE'RE NOT A TEAM WHOSE GOAL IS SIMPLY TO MAKE IT THROUGH THE DISTRICT PRIMARY.
I'M TALKING ABOUT THE WAKISAKA FIRST!
EVERY YEAR ONE TEAM USES ROUGH STUFF BECAUSE THEY DON'T ACTUALLY HAVE ANY ABILITY.
OUR GOAL IS THE TOKYO CHAMPIONSHIP AND NOTHING ELSE. WE CAN'T GET INJURED BEFORE THE REAL GAME BEGINS.
I WISH WEAK TEAMS PLAYED ONLY OTHER WEAK TEAMS.
FOR THE PRIMARY, WE'RE ONLY USING 30% OF OUR STRENGTH, SO IF YOU TRY HARD ENOUGH, YOU MIGHT BE ABLE TO DO WELL.
GOOD LUCK, JOSUI!

HEY --
MUSASHI-NOMORI PLAYED AGAINST US USING ALL THEIR STRENGTH.
WITH ONLY 30%, YOU CAN'T DEFEAT JOSUI.
THE WINNER'S NOT DETERMINED BY THE NAME OF THE SCHOOL.
LET'S GO.
Y-- YEAH ...
PAM!
NIPPON

DID YOU HEAR THAT? NO WAY MUSASHINOMORI USED ALL THEIR STRENGTH AGAINST THEM! WHAT A LIAR!
WE CAN'T BE FOOLED BY SOMEONE WITH BAND-AIDS ALL OVER HIS FACE!
HE MAKES ME LAUGH.
HA HA!
HAHAHAHAHA
HUMPH. JOSUI, JUST WATCH HOW THE GAME IS PLAYED.
YOU'LL SEE THE DIFFERENCE IN OUR STRENGTH.
AND YOU'LL PAY FOR WHAT YOU DID TO MY PREDATORS.
I'M SHOCKED.
SHŌ, SOMETIMES YOU SPEAK SO BOLDLY.
THOUGH USUALLY YOU'RE SO MILD.
REALLY?
WHY DON'T YOU SHOW THEM WHAT A WEAKLING CAN DO?
SLAP
YUP.
WHY DO YOU LOAD ME UP LIKE THIS?
KNOCK IT OFF. THIS WAS ALL YOUR FAULT.
FINALLY, TOMORROW, OUR BATTLE BEGINS.

STAGE.52 A Mighty Kick

HMMMM
OYASSAN!

HEY.

OVER HERE. HURRY.

SORRY I'M LATE.
HOW'S THE GAME?
!
KŌ-CHAN, WILL YOU HOLD ON TO THE OTHER SIDE?
TADAAAAHH

VOR! JOSUI JUNIOR HIGH SOCCER TEAM
A MIGHTY KICK

GO! GO!

WHAT'S WRONG? BE STRONG!

THOSE PLAYERS ARE UNKNOWN. WHAT DO YOU HAVE AGAINST THEM?

JOSUI
WHOOMP
HEY!
JOSUI
WAKISAKA FIRST
FIRST HALF
2
0
SECOND HALF
1
0
TOTAL
TAA-WAHHHHH!

THIS HAS GOTTA BE A JOKE.

WE'RE REGULARS IN THE TOKYO CHAMPIONSHIP, AND WE'RE UP AGAINST JOSUI?

THEY ALWAYS DROP OUT OF THE DISTRICT PRIMARY...

HMPH!

WHOOOSH
WE CAN'T LOSE...
... AGAINST THEM!
SKROOTCHH
FOOOM
NUTS!
WHOOSH
GET...
... OUT OF MY WAY.
CAPTAIN!

FOR THE SUMMER CHAMPIONSHIP
THE NO. 9 OF WAKISAKA FIRST--
FOR THE SUMMER CHAMPIONSHIP
HE'S GOT A 90% CHANCE ...
...HIS SHOT MAKES IT.
HE GOT THE BALL FREE. IT'S ONE-ON-ONE AGAINST THE GK!
HE'LL SCORE.
BAM
WAKISAKA

SLAMM
...HE'LL AIM AT THE NEAR-POST!
AH.
ONCE I'VE GOT THE DATA, THIS KIND OF SHOT IS...
WHISHHH
BAMM!
...NO PROBLEM AT ALL.

SNAP!
WHISHHH
GOOD JOB! PRETENDING TO TRAP, HE LET IT THROUGH!! THEN, SENT IT TO THE FRONTLINE!
BAM!

WHOOOOM
AT THE POST, SHIGEKI SENT THE BALL TO SHŌ!
VANISHED !?
GRRRR!
OOPS, THAT WAS CLOSE!
WHOOOM
WHOOM
GOOD JOB--THE KEEPER SAVED SHŌ.
HMM.
I CAN'T LET YOU SCORE SO MUCH --

HEH
PAM
AH.
AH.

WHOOMP
THUM
JOSUI
WAKISAKA FIRST
4-0
JOSU

YAAYY!♡
COOL!
JOSUI'S NO. 10 IS GREAT!

HEY, GIRLS! WHO ARE YOU FOR?
HUH
YOU SHOULD CHEER YOUR OWN SCHOOL'S TEAM!
WAKISAKA

JERK!
GRRRRRR
JEALOUS GUYS ARE SO LAME!
CAPTAIN, CALM DOWN!
'SIDES, EVEN IF WE CHEER YOU, IT'S ALREADY HOPELESS.
WE CAN'T EVEN TELL WHICH TEAM'S THE REGULAR MEMBER OF TOKYO CHAMPION-SHIP!
WAKISAKA

AREN'T YOU ASHAMED TO BE DOING SO BADLY AGAINST A LOWER RANK?
ONCE A MAN LOSES AGAINST OVER-WHELMING POWER, WHAT DOES HE DO?

EITHER HE GIVES UP, ACCEPTING HIS ABILITY, OR HE...
...KEEPS AT IT, DOING HIS BEST, NARROWING THE GAP BETWEEN HIS COMPETITION, AND TRIES TO WIN THE NEXT TIME.

JOSUI, WHO LOST AGAINST MUSASHINOMORI DURING THE SPRING CHAMPIONSHIP...

MA-SATO!

KRAKKK

JOSUI INTER-CEPTED AGAIN!

WHISHHH

...CHOSE THE LATTER.

BAMMMM

GO!

FWAPP
TOSUI
3
WHOOMP
WHY!?
WHY ARE WE LOSING AGAINST SUCH A SLAPDASH TEAM?
THEIR ATTITUDES ARE DIFFERENT.
THOSE SATISFIED WITH THE STATUS QUO WILL NEVER DEFEAT SHŌ'S TEAM, WHICH ALWAYS ASPIRES TO BE BETTER.
WE'RE NOT THE SAME TEAM WE WERE TWO MONTHS AGO.

THE NO.9 OF JOSUI VANISHED AGAIN!
NOT AGAIN.
THERE HE IS!
STOP THAT GUY!
EVERY YEAR ONE TEAM USES ROUGH STUFF BECAUSE THEY DON'T ACTUALLY HAVE ANY ABILITY.
I WISH WEAK TEAMS PLAYED ONLY OTHER WEAK TEAMS.
OUR GOAL IS THE TOKYO CHAMPIONSHIP AND NOTHING ELSE. WE CAN'T GET INJURED BEFORE THE REAL GAME BEGINS.
WITH ONLY 30%, YOU CAN'T DEFEAT JOSUI.
THE WINNER'S NOT DETERMINED BY THE NAME OF THE SCHOOL.
STOP HIM!
Y-- YEAH ...
GOOD LUCK, JOSUI!
FOR THE PRIMARY, WE'RE ONLY USING 30% OF OUR STRENGTH, SO IF YOU

THUMP
LOOK! HE TRIPPED SHŌ.
UNNHHHH
!
SHŌ, GO!

...BECAUSE I KNOW HOW AWFUL IT FEELS...
WHOOOSHH
I WON'T BE DEFEATED...

...TO LOSE AFTER DOING MY VERY BEST!

USING THAT FEELING TO PUSH US...
JOSUI
BAMMM!
...WE'VE BECOME STRONGER.

WHOOOMP

JOSUI WAKISAKA FIRST
6–0

THEY CAN'T BE JOSUI.
PLEASE TELL ME ISN'T HAPPENING.
IF IT'S A DREAM, WAKE ME UP...

WHISTLE!

STAGE.53

Confidence and Anxiety

HEY, YOU SEE THAT TOURNAMENT LIST?
TAIHEI THIRD
MUR-AYAMA FOURTH
JOSUI
IWASHI-MIZU

YOU KNOW ANYTHING ABOUT JOSUI? THEY JUST WON THE FIRST PLACE OF THE FOURTH BLOCK.
NOTHING.

THEY NEVER MADE IT INTO THE LEAGUE BEFORE, BUT I HEAR THEY'RE REALLY STRONG NOW.
THEY WON WITHOUT LETTING THEIR OPPONENTS SCORE A POINT.
AND THE TEAM SUPPOSEDLY CONSISTS MAINLY OF THE EIGHTH GRADERS.

WE CAN'T LOOK DOWN ON THEM.
SINCE THEY'RE EIGHTH GRADERS THAT MEANS THEY'LL SHOW UP AGAIN NEXT YEAR.
WE'D BETTER GET SOME DATA ON THEM.

MUSASHINOMORI PRIVATE SCHOOL

HEH ♡

SO WHAT ABOUT IT? ISN'T IT EXACTLY WHAT I TOLD YOU BEFORE, HUH, AKIRA? ♡

KNOCK IT OFF, SEIJI. THEY ONLY MADE IT THROUGH THE DISTRICT PRIMARY... I MEAN THE LEAGUE MATCH.

THEY'VE GOT TO WIN THROUGH THE TOURNAMENT BEFORE THEY'LL MAKE IT TO TOKYO CHAMPION-SHIP.

HUMPH!

WHO KNOWS HOW LONG THEIR LUCK WILL LAST? HOW MANY GAMES WILL THEY HAVE TO WIN BEFORE THEY PLAY AGAINST US?

I'M NOT SURE ABOUT YOUR ATTITUDE.

OH, SHUT UP AND GO AWAY!

Y'KNOW, THEY'RE ON THE RIGHT TRACK IN BUILDING THEIR TEAM.

MUSASHINOMORI PRIVATE SCHOOL GK CAPTAIN KATSURŌ SHIBUSAWA

ACCORDING TO SEIJI, BESIDES HAVING A GREAT COACH, THEY'VE GOT A NEW GK. THAT'S A LOT OF POWER.

I CAN'T WAIT TO PLAY AGAINST THEM...

IT'S LIKE MY TALENT WAS ASLEEP, BUT NOW IT'S BLOSSOMED. OR MAYBE THIS IS MY TRUE TALENT AFTER ALL.

WHAT-EVER, BIG GUY.

SHUT UP.

WHAT'S WRONG, YŪSUKE?

THINGS ARE GOING SO WELL, BUT I FEEL ALL WORRIED...

...LIKE THERE MIGHT BE THIS HUGE TRAP OR SOME-THING...

GEEZ! YOU'RE A WORRY-WART, AREN'T YOU?

WE'LL KEEP GOING AND REMEMBER THAT OUR GOAL IS BEATING MUSASHI-NOMORI!

THEN, WILL YOU TRANSLATE THE NEXT ONE?
WHOOSHH
UNH-HHH.
THWIPP
THWIIP
ZZZZZ...
ZZZZ...
NOTHING WAKES HIM UP...NOT EVEN MY RUBBER BAND.
ZZZZ...
WHAT FUN!
WHAT'RE YOU DOING?
I WANTED TO SEE WHAT IT TAKES TO WAKE HIM UP.
HA!
2-A

OH, IT'S YOU, ANE-SAN!
AREN'T YOU SUPPOSED TO CALL ME MS. KATORI?
I KNOW YOU'RE EXHAUSTED, BUT SOCCER PLAYERS NEED TO REMEMBER THAT THEIR MAIN JOB IS TO BE STUDENTS.
YOU'RE SLACKING OFF. GO STAND OUTSIDE.
IT'S YOUR FAULT.
2-B
C'MON, DON'T FALL ASLEEP, YOU MORON!
... THERE-FORE ...
...FOR THIS PROBLEM, USING THIS FORMULA ...

THERE'S NO PROBLEM IN OUR OFFENSE. FWS AND MIDDLE FIELDERS ARE WORKING WELL TOGETHER.
THE PROBLEM IS OUR DEFENSE. THE WAY IT IS NOW, WE WILL...
DF
TATSUYA.
IT WAS OBVIOUS IN THE DISTRICT PRIMARY THAT OUR GK AND OUR DFS DON'T WORK TOGETHER WELL. WE MANAGED TO KEEP OUR OPPONENT'S SCORE AT ZERO, BUT...
...I'M WORRIED WE'RE GOING TO BE FACING STRONGER TEAMS.
YEAH, I CONSIDERED THAT, TOO.
IN ONE WEEK, WE'LL BE RUSHING INTO A TOUR-NAMENT MATCH.
WE SHOULD DEAL WITH THAT BEFORE THEN.
HEY, TATSUYA!
PLEASANTLY CHATTING WITH YUKI? YOU SEEM RELAXED.
AND SINCE YOU ARE, WHY DON'T YOU SOLVE THE PROBLEM ON THE BLACK-BOARD?
YES, TEACHER.
IT'S TOO DIFFICULT. HE WON'T SOLVE THAT.
HE'S ACTING OUT OF SPITE 'CAUSE THE TEACHER ISN'T POPULAR.

WHOOM
IS THIS RIGHT?
SKRITCHH!

DING DING
YOU GOT IT.
HEH HEH
TATSUYA!
YAYYYY
SUCH A KNOW-IT-ALL.

SOCCER TEAM

YOU DON'T LOOK WELL, KOGA.

CAUSE I'M SO TIRED.
...YOU KNOW ...
YOU, TOO, YOSHI-HIKO.
YOU LOOK PALE.

READ THIS WAY
...RECENTLY...
...I'M NOT ENJOYING PLAYING.
I MEAN, I LIKE WINNING...
...BUT...

...HOW DO I EXPLAIN IT...? IT'S LIKE SHŌ'S IGNORING US...
HE'S BECOME SO DISTANT.

AND SOME-THING'S GOING ON WITH DAICHI.

FISHHHH
PUFFF
....

I COUNT ON YOU OVER THERE.
DEFENSE!
GO AROUND!

HUH
NORO! HE'S COMING FROM THE RIGHT. DRIVE HIM FROM OUTSIDE!
KAORU, THE LEFT!

WHUMP
WHAT'RE YOU DOING?
GET OUT! I CAN'T SEE THE BALL!
BOOM
PAMP!

WHOOOOMP

NUTS!

YOU'RE NOT ONLY SLOW, YOU DON'T FOLLOW DIRECTIONS.
DON'T YOU THINK IT WOULD BE BETTER IF YOU'RE REPLACED?
!
DA-ICHI!

DON'T YOU THINK SHIGEKI IS BETTER SUITED AS A GK THAN DAICHI?

THE ISSUE WITH THE RELATIONSHIP BETWEEN THE DFs AND THE GK HAD TO COME UP SOONER OR LATER.

IF NOTHING CROPPED UP, I WAS PREPARED TO START IT MYSELF.

THEY BRING OUT THE PROBLEMS AND FIND ANSWERS THEM-SELVES.

EVEN IF YOU HAVE NO BAD INTENTIONS, YOUR WORDS HURT THE OTHERS.
YOU DON'T WANT THEM TO MISUNDER-STAND YOU, DO YOU?
I...
...DON'T MIND.
SOCCER CAN'T BE PLAYED ALONE. IT'S A TEAM SPORT.
I KNOW YOU'RE INCREDIBLE, BUT YOU SHOULD THINK OF WHAT NORO AND THE OTHERS --
SHŌ!

I STILL DON'T UNDERSTAND WHY YOU'RE SMILING.
I FIND SOCCER AND BEING GK...
... ANY-THING BUT FUN.
I CAN'T UNDER-STAND YOU.
WHY ARE YOU SMILING?
TELL ME.
DAICHI ...
...I'M SORRY.
I DON'T KNOW WHAT TO SAY.

GK OF MUSA-SHINOMORI PRIVATE SCHOOL ...
KATS-URŌ.

I SUPPOSE IF IT WAS KATSURŌ, HE WOULD HAVE SAID SOMETHING WORTH-WHILE, BUT...

KATS-URŌ?
YOU REMEMBER SEIJI? HE VISITED THE OTHER DAY. HE'S A SENIOR IN THE SAME SCHOOL.
AMONG THE JUNIOR HIGHS, KATSURŌ IS A TOP CLASS GK.

THE FOLLOWING DAY.
WHAT?

WHERE'S DAICHI?

HE'S ABSENT WITHOUT A NOTE.
HE'S SUCH A MYSTERY.
...
I HAVE A FEELING ...
...HE MIGHT'VE GONE TO MUSASHI-NOMORI.
TAP TAP

SMALL WHISTLE! THEATRE

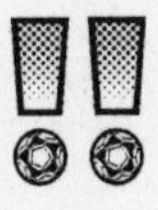

MANGA BY SEKI, ASSISTANT S

It's a secret. Part 1.

IF YOU DON'T GET IT, PLEASE READ VOLUME 4 ♥.

It's a secret. Part 2.

Soccer Fairy

SHE CHARMS THE SOCCER BOY'S HEART.

"Whistle!" Production Staff.

As of 1999.

MAINLY IN CHARGE OF FINALIZING.

PLUS THE HEAD COOK OF THE FAMILY. GREAT TONER. NO ONE CAN MATCH HER SKILL.

PLUS IN CHARGE OF THE MOB. HIGUCHI GROUP'S MASCOT OR RATHER, EVERYONE LIKES TO TEASE HER.

SHE'S KNOWN HIGUCHI FOR ABOUT TEN YEARS. SHE CAN DO ANYTHING, AND HER ABILITY TO SUPPORT IS TREMENDOUS.

THE AUTHOR

MAINLY IN CHARGE OF THE BACKGROUND AND THE EFFECT LINES.

MAINLY IN CHARGE OF THE BACKGROUND.

URRGH

UTADA

BATMAN ♡

HEH...

HIGUCHI-SAN, WE'RE IN TROUBLE.

IT'S NICE TO HAVE BEAUTIFUL THINGS.

Assistant S

Meso Aiko

Assistant T

Higuchi

Assistant N

Assistant M

Next in Whistle!

STEP BY STEP

Even when it means kicking ball with people you would never kick around with, Shô Kazamatsuri understands the concept of teamwork and won't quit until he leads Josui Junior High to victory!

The rest of Josui's squad, however, is still grappling with what it really means to be a team. With all the infighting and griping going on, Josui will have a hard time beating Iwa Tech, an opponent that takes pride in its impenetrable line of defense. Can Shô's crew finally put their individual differences aside to form a unified team?

Available September 2005!

WHO WILL PLAY AKIRA--
HIKARU OR SAI?

only $7.95 each

www.shonenjump.com

Also available at your local bookstore, comic store and Suncoast Motion Picture Company.